C-SUITE CHEMISTRY

THE KEY TO BUILDING HIGH-PERFORMING TEAMS

CHRISTOPHER HOLMES

CONTENTS

CHAPTER ONE

UNDERSTANDING THE C-SUITE CHEMISTRY

C-suite, or C-level, is a widely-used vernacular describing the upper echelons of a corporation's senior executives and managers.

C-suite gets its name from the titles of top senior executives, which tend to start with the letter C, for "chief," as in chief executive officer (CEO), chief financial officer (CFO), chief operating officer (COO), and chief information officer (CIO) (CIO).

MAIN POINTS

- "C-suite" refers to the executive-level managers within a company.
- Common c-suite executives include the chief executive officer (CEO), chief financial officer (CFO), chief operating officer (COO), and chief information officer (CIO) (CIO).
- C-level members work together to ensure a company stays true to its established plans and policies.
- Historically there are more males in C-Suite jobs than women.
- C-suite execs often work long hours and have high-stress jobs, but usually, these jobs come with extremely lucrative compensation packages.

The C-suite is generally the most significant and influential group of employees inside a firm. Reaching this high level often demands a lot of experience and finely-honed leadership qualities. While many C-level executives formerly relied on functional know-how and technical skills to climb the lower rungs of the corporate ladder, most have cultivated more visionary perspectives needed to make sound upper-management decisions.

The CEO, CFO, and COO most frequently come to mind when talking about the C-suite. However, several other positions fall into this executive level. Other C-Suite officers include:

- Chief Compliance Officer (CCO) (CCO)
- Chief Human Resources Manager (CHRM) (CHRM)
- Chief Security Officer (CSO) (CSO)
- Chief Green Officer (CGO) (CGO)
- Chief Analytics Officer (CAO) (CAO)
- Chief Marketing Officer (CMO) (CMO)
- Chief Data Officer (CDO) (CDO)
- Chief Executive Officer (CEO) (CEO)

Invariably the highest-level corporate executive, the CEO, traditionally serves as the face of the company and frequently consults other C-suite members for advice on major decisions. CEOs may come from any professional experience, as long as they have established strong leadership and decision-making abilities throughout their career trajectories.

Chief Financial Officer (CFO) (CFO)
The CFO position represents the top of the corporate ladder for financial analysts and accountants striving for upward mobility in the financial industry. Portfolio management, accounting, investment research, and financial analysis are the prime skills that CFOs must possess. CFOs have global mindsets and work closely with CEOs to source new business opportunities while weighing each potential venture's financial risks and benefits.

Chief Information Officer (CIO) (CIO)
A leader in information technology, the CIO normally begins as a business analyst, and then moves for C-level status while building technical abilities in fields like programming, coding, project management, and mapping. CIOs are generally competent at applying these functional abilities to risk management, corporate strategy, and finance tasks. In many firms, CIOs may also be referred to as the chief technology officers (CTOs), but other companies may host both roles.

The number of C-level roles varies based on factors including the size, purpose, and industry of a firm. Smaller businesses may just need a COO to manage human resources operations, but bigger businesses may need both a CHRM and a COO.
Chief Operating Officer (COO) The COO oversees a company's operations and serves as the HR C-level executive. They concentrate on things like hiring, training, paying employees, and providing legal and

administrative services. The COO often serves as the CEO's deputy.

Director of Marketing (CMO)

The CMO often advances to the C-suite from positions in sales or marketing. These executives are adept at leading product development and social innovation activities across physical locations and online platforms, the latter of which is crucial in the current digital age.

Director of Technology (CTO)

The executive in charge of an organization's technical requirements as well as its research and development is known as the chief technology officer (CTO) (R&D). This person, often referred to as a chief technical officer, analyzes an organization's short- and long-term requirements and uses the money to make investments meant to aid the business in achieving its goals. Typically, the chief executive officer (CEO) of the company receives direct reports from the CTO.

C-level members collaborate to guarantee that a company's strategy and operations are in line with its set plans and rules. When it comes to public corporations, C-level management staff frequently rectify actions that don't seem to improve revenues for shareholders.
Executives in the C-suite have demand, for high-stakes jobs and are often compensated well.

Dealing with a range of stakeholder personalities is unavoidable for a C-level executive. Most of the time, how we connect with people affects our likelihood of succeeding in reaching our objectives. You don't need to worry any longer if this information regarding relationship complications disturbs you.

A single personality test is not all that Business Chemistry is. Instead, it is a framework that identifies the Driver, the Pioneer, the Integrator, and the Guardian as the four primary behavioural aspects.

The Driver(Operator)
They are intellectually creative and analytical thinkers.
Theorization is less enticing than experimentation.
They are determined, realistic, and task-oriented.
The needs of others and the human aspect might be overlooked.
They occasionally put themselves under a lot of work.

The Pioneer(First)
They like debating concepts and challenging the norm.
They seldom ever do the same thing in the same manner because of habitual boredom.
They are impulsive, adaptable, and flexible.
They may raise the mood of the whole group since they are encouraging and enthusiastic.
For the sake of their ideals, they could disregard practical considerations.

The Integrator
They are in favour of environmental harmony.
They take their time resolving conflicts and taking into account everyone's perspectives.
They are cooperative, kind, and empathic.

They may support the rest of the group and mediate disputes.

They may get overburdened because they cannot say "no."

The Guardian

Although they are interested in cause and effect, they may place an excessive amount of emphasis on facts.

They can efficiently organize and analyze data using logical approaches.

Before taking action, they often consider several options.

They methodically and rationally accomplish what has to be done.

Fear of instability may prevent people from making changes.

Understanding the fundamentals may help you establish personal connections and, more crucially, dispel preconceived notions about how to interact with others. The Platinum Rule will replace the Golden Rule (treat others as you would want to be treated) (treat others as they wish to be treated). If you know how to make it happen, such abridgement may bring about a significant positive impact on the company climate.

Senior staff often lead their team based on either their natural talent or experience, which may lead to inconsistent performance. We should first conduct a team analysis to close the gap. Consider the following inquiries:

What components make up my team?

How can I leverage those components to encourage

teamwork and, on a larger scale, organizational engagement?

Or, when confronted with a specific task, C-level executives should begin by:

What qualifications does this job need? Which one is already on my team?

Is each member's element appropriate for the tasks at hand?

How is the job process assessed by each component?

You should show your team members the blind areas each person cannot see and provide them with coverings now that you have your team profile at your disposal. Avoid giving them jobs that will play to their weaknesses as well.

With Drivers on your squad, you have to

Make them extensively debate issues with others before making a choice. Encourage them to pay attention to and consider other people's perspectives.

Keep them from taking on too much work.

relieve them of diplomatic duties

teach kids leadership skills like diplomacy and tact

Pioneers, keep in mind to:

Pay attention to the information they overlook

Keep reminding them of due dates and minute consequences of their conduct.

Instead of routine jobs, give them innovative ones.

Teach them how to manage their time

Integrators' Covers include:

Aid them in setting priorities for their duties.
Give them precise due dates and regular reminders.
Sometimes steer children clear of interpersonal disputes
Teach them how to manage their time

Guardians function best if you:

Encourage them to look into more knowledge sources, particularly social ones.
Using examples and verified data, discuss why changes are important and beneficial.
Participate in planning processes with them, including risk management
To make them more receptive, invite them to meetings and brainstorming sessions.
Despite the components' diversity, not every one of them fits neatly into a single category. Instead, the majority of individuals are a combination of the two, enabling them to call upon secondary features as needed.

Identification of who you are and who you are working with is no longer that confusing when using the four aforementioned criteria as a guide. What matters most right now is how CFOs can use the solutions to create a communication strategy with proven results!

CHAPTER TWO

CREATING RAPPORT AND TRUST IN THE C-SUITE

The importance of building trust and rapport among C-Suite executives has increased due to the fast-changing nature of the corporate environment today. Building rapport and trust among C-suite executives is crucial for efficient decision-making and the success of the firm as a whole. Lack of trust and cooperation among CEOs may result in failures in communication, competing goals, and a lack of responsibility. The financial success of the business, staff morale, and customer satisfaction may all suffer as a result.

The following are important techniques for fostering rapport and trust among C-suite executives:

Establish clear channels of communication: Effective and frequent communication amongst C-Suite executives is crucial. Regular meetings or conference calls may be necessary, along with the open and honest sharing of company objectives and goals.

Create a collaborative environment by encouraging the C-Suite to function as a team to accomplish organizational objectives. To overcome issues and accomplish shared goals, leaders should be prepared to listen to one another.

Accept a common vision: The organization's executives

should be united by a common vision. This might include deciding on a shared set of values and goals, as well as identifying clear goals and priorities.

Encourage a variety of thinking since it may lead to the discovery of fresh possibilities and innovative solutions for issues. C-suite executives should be encouraged to provide many viewpoints and ideas, and they should be receptive to criticism and feedback that is offered constructively.

Encourage accountability and transparency: When everyone in the C-Suite is responsible for their actions, a culture of trust is established. As a result, CEOs need to be ready to own up to their errors, accept accountability for their actions, and keep one another responsible.

Invest in team-building exercises: These exercises may assist to improve communication and cooperation among executives. These might be less formal—like retreats or training sessions—or more formal—like group meals or social gatherings.

Recognize and reward accomplishments: It's critical to thank CEOs for their work when they reach goals and objectives. This may support encouraging good conduct and a culture of cooperation and teamwork.

It takes time and works to build rapport and trust among C-Suite executives, but the benefits are great. The C-Suite can accomplish shared objectives, make smarter choices, and create a culture of trust and responsibility by working together as a team. C-Suite leaders may collaborate to build a high-performing company that can handle any situation with good communication, clear objectives, and a readiness to accept other viewpoints.

CHAPTER THREE

COMMUNICATION TACTICS FOR THE C-SUITE

Effective communication is essential for any business to succeed, but it is much more important at the C-Suite level. C-Suite executives need to be able to communicate clearly with one another and with staff members at all organizational levels. For this, communication must be considered carefully and strategically, taking into consideration the special possibilities and problems encountered by executives at the top echelons of a business.

Here are some essential tactics for C-Suite communication success:

Be succinct and clear: C-suite executives are time-constrained and very busy. When speaking with other executives, it's crucial to be direct, straightforward, and swift to the point. Creating concise summaries or executive briefings that highlight important details and priorities can be one way to achieve this.

Customize your communication style: Executives communicate in a variety of ways. While some people may prefer phone conversations or in-person meetings, others could choose email or instant messaging. To achieve efficient communication, it's critical to adjust your communication style to each executive's preferences.

Actively listening is a crucial component of effective communication, in addition to speaking. Executives in the C-suite should practice active listening to one another and workers at all organizational levels. This entails being receptive to suggestions and inquiries, as well as challenging assumptions.

Manage contradictory information: In the C-Suite, executives often get conflicting information from several sources. It's critical to handle these competing signals by determining the information's trustworthiness and source, as well as by speaking with other executives to clear up any misunderstanding or ambiguity.

Keep everything transparent: Building rapport and confidence inside the C-Suite requires open and honest communication. Executives should be willing to share information with staff members at all levels of the business. They should also be open and honest about their goals and decision-making procedures.

Use data and analytics: To guide their decisions and successfully collaborate with other executives, C-Suite executives should use data and analytics. This might entail highlighting important metrics and trends using dashboards or other visualizations, as well as leveraging data to back up claims and suggestions.

Tell the audience why: Executives in the C-Suite must explain why something needs to be done in addition to what needs to be done. To achieve this, it is important to be clear about the strategic goals and objectives that guide organizational decision-making and to make sure that all executives support these objectives.

The success of the C-Suite depends on effective communication, but it can be difficult. Executives at this level must be able to effectively communicate with people from a variety of backgrounds and viewpoints while navigating a complex web of relationships and priorities. C-Suite executives can create strong relationships, promote organizational success, and motivate their teams to succeed by being clear and concise, adapting their communication style, listening actively, managing conflicting messages, upholding transparency, using data and analytics, and communicating the why.

CHAPTER FOUR

RESOLUTION OF DISPUTES IN THE C-SUITE

Working in any firm always involves conflict, and the C-Suite is no exception. Managing disagreements at the C-Suite level may be especially difficult given the high stakes and intricate connections involved. The C-Suite demands thorough and strategic conflict resolution that takes into consideration the particular dynamics of this level of the business.

Here are some essential techniques for C-Suite dispute resolution that work:

Determine the conflict's underlying cause: Different strategic goals, personal or professional disagreements, misunderstandings or miscommunications, and other factors may all lead to conflicts in the C-Suite. To create a plan for resolving the dispute, it is essential to determine its underlying causes.

Encourage honest communication Conflict resolution in the C-Suite requires open and honest communication. The open and honest expression of concerns and opinions, as well as active listening to those of other executives, should be promoted among executives.

Gaining the confidence and respect of others is essential to settling disagreements in the C-Suite. To identify common ground and handle disputes cooperatively, executives who respect and trust one another are more likely to be able to do so.

Create a resolution plan: It's critical to create a resolution strategy when the conflict's underlying causes have been determined and open lines of communication and trust have been established. This can include formulating a list of potential solutions, weighing the advantages and disadvantages of each choice, and deciding on the best course of action in light of the demands and goals of the company.

Practice attentive listening: A key element of successful dispute resolution is active listening. This entails paying close attention to the worries and viewpoints of other executives, getting clarification via questioning, and summarizing the main ideas to make sure that everyone is on the same page.

Concentrate on the organization's goals: In the C-Suite, disagreements that have nothing to do with the goals of the company may occasionally develop from personal or professional issues. When settling disputes, it's crucial to keep the organization's interests in mind and refrain from letting disagreements over personal or professional matters influence judgment.

Create roles and duties that are clear: By ensuring that everyone is aware of their place in the decision-making process, clear roles and duties may reduce disputes in the C-Suite. Establishing distinct lines of authority and responsibility as well as defining the protocols and processes for decision-making will help with this.

If required, seek outside assistance: Conflicts in the C-Suite may sometimes be complicated to settle. It can be required under certain circumstances to enlist the assistance of a mediator or conflict resolution professional who can aid in facilitating dialogue and directing the resolution process.

The C-Suite's success depends on its ability to resolve disputes effectively. C-Suite executives can effectively manage conflicts and create strong, collaborative relationships that support organizational success by identifying the root causes of disagreements, encouraging open communication, establishing trust and rapport, developing a resolution strategy, practising active listening, concentrating on the organization's interests, defining clear roles and responsibilities, and, if necessary, seeking outside assistance.

CHAPTER FIVE

LEADERSHIP STYLES IN THE C-SUITE

L eadership styles play a critical role in shaping team dynamics and determining the success of a team. There are several different leadership styles, each with its own strengths and weaknesses. In this book, we will discuss the most common leadership styles and their impact on team dynamics.

Autocratic Leadership
Autocratic leadership is characterized by a single leader who makes decisions for the team without consulting with or considering input from other team members. This style of leadership can be effective in situations where quick decisions need to be made or when the leader possesses specific knowledge or expertise that is necessary for the success of the team. However, it can also create resentment and frustration among team members who feel left out of the decision-making process.

Democratic Leadership
Democratic leadership involves the leader soliciting input and feedback from team members before making a decision. This style of leadership can be effective in situations where multiple perspectives are needed to

make an informed decision or when team members have specialized knowledge or expertise. It can lead to more buy-in and engagement from team members, and can help to build a strong team culture. However, it can also be time-consuming and may result in slower decision-making processes.

Transformational Leadership

Transformational leadership is characterized by a leader who inspires and motivates team members to achieve a common goal. This style of leadership can be effective in situations where a team is working toward a challenging goal or where individual team members need to be encouraged to perform at their highest level. It can lead to a strong sense of shared purpose and can foster innovation and creativity. However, it can also be difficult to sustain over the long term and may not be effective in situations where clear direction or guidance is needed.

Servant Leadership

Servant leadership is characterized by a leader who prioritizes the needs of team members over their own needs. This style of leadership can be effective in situations where team members need support or guidance to achieve their goals, or when team members are facing challenges that require a supportive and caring leader. It can lead to increased trust and respect between team members and the leader, and can foster a positive team culture. However, it may not be effective in situations where clear direction or strong leadership is needed.

Laissez-Faire Leadership

Laissez-faire leadership is characterized by a hands-off approach where the leader provides minimal guidance or direction to the team. This style of leadership can be effective in situations where team members have a high level of autonomy or where individual team members have specialized knowledge or expertise. However, it can also lead to confusion and lack of direction, and can result in decreased motivation and engagement among team members.

The impact of leadership styles on team dynamics can be significant. A leader who uses an autocratic style of leadership may create a culture of fear or resentment, while a democratic leader may create a culture of collaboration and engagement. A transformational leader may inspire innovation and creativity, while a servant leader may foster a culture of care and support.

In order to create effective team dynamics, it is important for a leader to understand the strengths and weaknesses of each leadership style and to adapt their style to the needs of the team and the situation. This may involve using a combination of different leadership styles or adapting a specific leadership style to meet the needs of individual team members or projects.

In conclusion, leadership styles play a critical role in shaping team dynamics and determining the success of a team. Understanding the strengths and weaknesses of each leadership style can help leaders to create a positive team culture that fosters engagement, motivation, and collaboration. By adapting their leadership style to meet the needs of the team and the situation, leaders can create a strong and successful team that achieves its goals and drives organizational success.

CHAPTER SIX

DECISION-MAKING IN THE C-SUITE

Making decisions is essential to the success of a business in the C-Suite. C-Suite executives choices may have a significant impact on the whole firm and its stakeholders. Therefore, effective and informed decision-making in the C-Suite is crucial.
We'll talk about the main variables that affect executive-level decision-making as well as the best strategies for making wise choices.

Information: The C-Suite needs access to current, accurate information to make effective decisions. This might consist of financial information, market trends, consumer insights, and other pertinent information. To make wise judgments, executives must be able to evaluate and comprehend this data. Executives must have access to the finest data accessible since the reliability and quality of the information provided may have a big influence on the decision-making process.

Collaboration is essential for successful decision-making among C-Suite leaders. Executive collaboration is crucial to ensuring that choices are in line with the organization's overall strategic objectives since decisions often include many departments and functions. Collaboration also makes it possible to make well-informed judgments that take into consideration many opinions and perspectives.

Risk management: Knowledge of the risks connected to each choice is necessary for the C-Suite to make effective decisions. Executives must analyze a decision's possible advantages and disadvantages before making a choice. To prevent the business from being exposed to unneeded risks or liabilities, risk management must be included in the decision-making process.

Strong leadership is necessary for the C-Suite to make effective decisions. The team has to be given direction and guidance by the leader, who must also make sure that choices are in line with the organization's overarching objectives. Collaboration, communication, and accountability are critical elements of good decision-making, and effective leadership promotes these elements.

C-Suite executives should use data-driven decision-making rather than their gut feelings or preconceived notions. This makes judgments more likely to be fact-based and objectively reached. A culture that values data and is prepared to question presumptions and personal biases, as well as access to trustworthy data and analytic tools, is necessary for data-driven decision-making.

Agile decision-making in the C-Suite requires the capacity to adjust to shifting conditions. The ability to react swiftly and efficiently to shifting market circumstances, new trends or other disturbances is a must for executives. This calls for flexibility and the capacity to modify plans and tactics as necessary.

Best Practices for the C-Effective Suite's Decision-

Making:

Define the issue precisely: Clarifying the situation is the first step in making decisions that will be successful. This makes it easier to make sure the choice is in line with the organization's overarching strategic objectives and tackles the problem's underlying causes.

Possibilities research and evaluation: Before making a choice, executives should research and assess many options. This makes it possible to make educated decisions that take into consideration many opinions and perspectives.

The possible risks and advantages of each solution should be considered by executives. Understanding the possible effects of each choice and being able to properly manage risk is necessary for this.

Include important parties: Key stakeholders should be included in the decision-making process. This makes it possible for the company to successfully manage stakeholder relationships and guarantee that choices are in line with stakeholders' demands and expectations.

Follow up on and assess outcomes: Monitoring and assessing the outcomes are necessary for effective decision-making. This makes it possible for the company to make successful judgments and change its strategy and goals as necessary.

In conclusion, the success of a business depends on the C-ability Suite to make wise decisions. important elements that affect

CHAPTER SEVEN

ORGANISATIONAL CULTURE AND THE C-SUITE

An organization's organizational culture refers to its common values, beliefs, and practices that influence how its employees behave. An organization's culture may have a big influence on how successful it is, and the C-Suite is essential to creating and preserving that culture. We'll talk about how C-Suite leaders may influence and mould the culture of their company as well as the connection between organizational culture and the C-Suite.

Through several factors, including leadership behaviour, decision-making procedures, communication, and incentive systems, organizational culture is formed and maintained. All of these processes are significantly influenced by the C-Suite, which means that it may significantly affect company culture. The C-Suite is in charge of establishing the organization's tone and direction, and their actions and choices have a big impact on the culture of the company.

Leadership conduct is one of the most important ways that the C-Suite may affect corporate culture. Individuals inside the business may behave differently depending on the C-communication Suite's style, decision-making procedures, and problem-solving methodology. For instance, if the C-Suite prioritizes open communication and transparency, this is likely to show in the actions of staff members across the board. The opposite is equally likely to be true if the C-Suite is mainly concerned with short-term earnings and does not place a high priority on ethical conduct.

The C-Suite may also have an impact on corporate culture through how they make decisions. The values and procedures of the firm may be significantly impacted by the choices made by the C-Suite. For instance, the C-Suite is likely to make choices that reflect those principles if it values inclusivity and cooperation. Similarly to this, the C-Suite is likely to take actions that support risk-taking and innovation if such values are important to them.

The C-Suite has a big part to play in this area since communication is a key element in determining company culture. To make sure that the values and objectives of the firm are recognized and upheld, the C-Suite must effectively communicate with the workforce, stakeholders, and the general public. While ineffective communication may result in uncertainty and distrust, effective communication can foster a feeling of purpose and alignment within the business.

The C-Suite may also affect corporate culture by putting in place incentive schemes. The C-Suite is in charge of creating and putting into place these systems, which may be used to reward and incentivize certain behaviours and practices. For instance, the C-Suite may put in place a reward structure that motivates staff to come up with fresh ideas and take calculated risks if they value innovation and risk-taking.

The C-Suite must be purposeful in their choices and behaviours if they want to create and sustain a healthy company culture. They must understand the company's beliefs and objectives and seek to ensure that these values are represented in all facets of the operations of the business. This requires a dedication to openness, teamwork, and moral conduct, as well as a readiness to modify and adjust as necessary.

Creating a clear set of company values and objectives and effectively communicating them to all stakeholders are among the best techniques for influencing organizational culture in the C-Suite.

Setting a good example and ensuring that the C-Suite behaves in a way that is compatible with the organization's values and objectives.
Encouraging group work and inclusivity in decision-making, as well as respecting other points of view.
Establishing a rewards system that supports the desired actions and practices and is consistent with the organization's beliefs and objectives.
Creating an environment where learning and adaptability are valued, and being open to changing course when necessary to get the results you want.

CHAPTER EIGHT

MANAGING CHANGE IN THE C-SUITE

The C-Suite has a crucial role to play in this area. An organization's success or failure may depend on its capacity to adjust and react to changes in the market, industry, or regulatory environment. In this chapter, we'll talk about the difficulties in managing change in the C-Suite as well as the best methods and approaches for doing so.

Any firm might find managing change challenging, but the C-Suite faces especially significant obstacles. Executives in the C-suite sometimes have large stakes in the status quo and may be averse to change. Additionally, it may be challenging to coordinate and align efforts around a single objective due to the high degree of specialization and compartmentalization of roles in the C-Suite. Implementing change in a timely and efficient way may be challenging due to these issues.

Despite these difficulties, there are several tactics and best practices that can assist C-Suite executives in successfully managing change. Communication is one of the most significant of these. Employees, stakeholders and the larger community must be effectively communicated with for them to understand why change is necessary and what the change will involve. Executives in the C-suite must be able to communicate successfully with a range of parties, including staff members, clients, investors, and regulatory agencies.

Engaging people in the process is a crucial element of change management. Employee involvement and feedback may be crucial in ensuring that changes are well-received and successful since they often have the biggest influence on the business. Executives in the C-suite should solicit and take into account the opinions of workers at all organizational levels and utilize these opinions to guide the change management process.

Making sure the change is in line with the organization's overarching vision and objectives is another crucial aspect of change management. It is important to convey the change in the context of attaining the organization's objectives. The change should also be in line with the organization's principles and culture, according to C-suite executives. This may guarantee that the change is welcomed and accepted by the stakeholders, including the staff.

Having a concise and well-defined strategy is essential for managing change. The change's goals, the actions needed to get there, and the timetable for execution should all be laid out in the plan. Additionally, the strategy must clearly define roles and effectively include all parties in its dissemination. This can make sure that the change is carried out in a planned and efficient way.

Last but not least, it's critical to give employees resources and support throughout the change management process. Change can be stressful and challenging, and employees may need extra help and resources to adjust to the changes. Throughout the change management process, C-suite executives should work to build a culture that values and supports employees and be ready to offer this support.

A well-defined plan, clear communication, employee participation, alignment with organizational goals and values, and support for employees are all necessary for successfully managing change in the C-Suite. C-Suite executives can successfully manage change and position their organizations for success in a rapidly changing business environment by adhering to these best practices and strategies.

Leadership behaviour, decision-making procedures, communication, and reward systems are just a few of the many ways that organizational culture is developed and maintained. All of these mechanisms are greatly influenced by the C-Suite, and as a result, the C-Suite can greatly influence organizational culture. The C-Suite is in charge of establishing the organization's tone and direction, and they have a big impact on the culture of the company through their actions and decisions.

Through their leadership actions, the C-Suite can significantly affect organizational culture. Individuals within the organization may behave differently depending on how the C-Suite behaves, including how they communicate, make decisions, and solve problems. For instance, if the C-Suite prioritizes openness and transparency, this is likely to show in how employees behave across the board. However, if the C-Suite is primarily concerned with short-term profits and does not place a high value on ethical behaviour, this is also likely to show in the behaviour of employees.

Through their method of decision-making, the C-Suite can also affect organizational culture. The C-decisions Suite can have a big impact on the organization's values and procedures. For instance, if the C-Suite values inclusivity and collaboration, they are more likely to make decisions that align with those values. Likewise, the C-Suite is likely to take actions that promote innovation and risk-taking if it shares those values.

Organizational culture is shaped by a variety of factors, including communication, and the C-Suite has a key role to play in this regard. To make sure that the company's values and goals are accepted and understood by all parties, the C-Suite must effectively communicate with its workforce, stakeholders, and the general public. In contrast to poor communication, which can result in confusion and mistrust, effective communication can contribute to the development of a sense of purpose and alignment within the organization.

Finally, the C-Suite can affect organizational culture by implementing reward systems. The C-Suite is in charge of developing and implementing systems that reward and incentivize employees to promote particular behaviours and practices. For instance, if the C-Suite values innovation and calculated risk-taking, they might put in place a compensation scheme that motivates staff to come up with fresh concepts and take calculated risks.

The C-Suite needs to be deliberate in its actions and choices if they want to create and keep a healthy organizational culture. They must be aware of the organization's values and objectives, and they must work to ensure that these values are reflected in every facet of its operations. This calls for a dedication to openness, teamwork, and moral conduct as well as the flexibility to change and adapt as necessary.

A clear set of organizational values and goals that are effectively communicated to all stakeholders is one of the best ways for the C-Suite to shape organizational culture.

By setting an example, the C-Suite can ensure that its actions are in line with the company's values and objectives.

encouraging group work, being inclusive, respecting different points of view when making decisions

designing a rewards system that supports the desired actions and practices and is in line with the objectives of the organization.

promoting a culture of learning and adaptation, as well as being prepared to veer off course when necessary to achieve the desired results.

CHAPTER NINE

DIVERSITY, EQUALITY AND INCLUSION IN THE C-SUITE

A company must have diversity, equality, and inclusion (DEI) to be successful and flourish. This chapter will cover the significance of DEI in the C-Suite as well as tactics for effectively adopting and promoting DEI. The C-Suite is a key player in determining the DEI culture of a business.

The significance of DEI in the C-Suite must first be understood. A diverse C-Suite may provide a variety of viewpoints, experiences, and talents, which can encourage innovation and creativity inside the company. Additionally, a diverse C-Suite may support the development of trust and engagement among staff members, clients, and other stakeholders as well as position the business as an industry leader.

However, variety on its own is insufficient. Focusing on fairness and inclusion is essential if DEI is to fully benefit society. No of their history or identity, equity entails ensuring that everyone has access to the same opportunities and resources. Making a culture where everyone feels appreciated, respected, and supported is a key component of inclusion.

So how can the C-Suite advance DEI throughout the company? Several tactics may be successful, including:

Clear and quantifiable DEI objectives should be established by the C-Suite, and members of the C-Suite should be held responsible for accomplishing these goals. This may guarantee that DEI is a top priority and is included in the organization's overarching plan.

Promote an inclusive culture: The C-Suite should try to establish an environment that appreciates and encourages inclusiveness. This might include giving workers the chance to express their opinions and experiences, encouraging polite and open dialogue, and offering tools and assistance to those from underrepresented groups.

The C-Suite should invest in DEI training for themselves as well as for all of the company's workers. This may aid in increasing knowledge and understanding of DEI concerns and in fostering an inclusive and respectful culture.

Develop a variety of networks: The C-Suite should try to develop a variety of partners and connections for these networks. This may enable the organization to establish itself as a pioneer in DEI and provide fresh viewpoints and ideas.

Holding leaders responsible: The C-Suite should be responsible for supporting and promoting DEI on their behalf as well as on behalf of other leaders within the company. Setting expectations for behaviour and encouraging responsibility for reaching DEI objectives might be part of this.

In conclusion, DEI is essential to an organization's

performance and long-term viability. The C-Suite is crucial to advancing DEI and should concentrate on establishing clear objectives, encouraging an inclusive culture, funding DEI training, creating diverse networks, and holding leaders responsible.

The C-Suite can position its company as a leader in DEI and encourage innovation, creativity, and participation throughout the whole business by implementing these methods.

FREQUENTLY ASKED QUESTIONS

What Jobs Are Included in the C-Suite?
The senior management roles inside a firm are referred to as the "C-suite," where the "C" stands for "chief." The C-suite is home to several chief officers, including the CEO, CIO, CFO, and others. Despite being well-compensated and powerful supervisors, these people are still working for the company. The number of C-level roles varies from business to company, based on elements including size, purpose, and industry.

Are Most C-Suite Executives Men?
Yes. Historically, only men occupied top management positions in firms. Over the past few decades, this has changed a bit. Still, a 2021 McKinsey & Company report found that women hold less than 25% of C-Suite positions.
Among Fortune 500 companies, only 8.2% are female CEOs.

How Can One Start a Career That Ends in the C-Suite?

There isn't a standard road map for reaching the C-suite. For some, being proactive and thoughtful about formulating your career path will be essential, while others may get by simply by being aggressive and rubbing elbows with the right people. In any case, hard work and a skilled track record are a must, and there's no room for complacency. Having proper credentials such as an MBA from a top business school is also a plus.

What Is Below the C-Suite?
The organizational structure of a company will vary, but typically the level below the C-Suite will feature top managers such as managing directors, senior vice presidents (SVPs), and division heads.

Which Is the Highest-Paid C-Suite Position?
According to Salary.com, the highest-paid C-Suite positions in 2021 were:

CEO - $754,700 (median salary)
COO - $457,500
CFO - $363,500
CIO/CTO - $250,000 CMO - $233,750